MAGIC SPELLS
AND
INCANTATIONS

MAGIC SPELLS AND INCANTATIONS

with an Introduction and Notes by

ELIZABETH PEPPER

The Witches' Almanac, Ltd.

Publishers   Newport

Address all inquiries and information to
THE WITCHES' ALMANAC, LTD.
P.O. Box 289
Tiverton, RI 02878

ISBN: 1-881098-21-4

First Printing October 2001

Printed in the United States of America

*Magic has power to experience and fathom things
which are inaccessible to human reason.
For magic is a great secret wisdom; and reasoning
against it is nothing else but extreme folly.*

— PARACELSUS, *De Occulta Philosophia*

CONTENTS

ILLUSTRATIONS

Cover art and chapter heads are adapted from the work of Aubrey Beardsley. In his brief life (1872-1898), the English graphic artist produced a remarkable series of designs and illustrations displaying his mastery of the balance between black and white, positive and negative space — a visual presentation of a magical theme.

Among the drawings and designs are works of many unknown artists from 15th-century woodcuts to 20th-century illustrations. All significant historical credits are referenced below.

Introduction

Spells and incantations have ever played a role in the drama of human life on Earth. Our most primitive cultures sensed that language had the power to lift spirits, free imagination, inspire hope, and lend courage. For over five thousand years, a treasury of hymns, rhymes, mystical words and phrases have graced the annals of Western magic. Words of power written on tomb walls in ancient Egypt, sacred books of Europe, folk legends, and nursery verses yield a wondrous variety of means by which the anxiety of human experience may be eased or erased.

The recitation of spells and charms should be at a tempo much slower than ordinary speech. We are told that the effect should be one of quiet emphasis and certain intent. Some say that the sound should be loud and clear; others recommend a whisper. Another source insists that the words be musically intoned. The words "charm" and "chant" derive from Latin, meaning "song." Shakespeare's Titania in *A Midsummer Night's Dream* advises:

> *First, rehearse your song by rote,*
> *To each word a warbling note:*
> *Hand in hand, with fairy grace,*
> *Will we sing, and bless this place.*

The river of magical traditions in the West flows from two primary sources and often intermingles to form a bewildering number of tributaries. Thoth, Egypt's god of words, governs esoteric rites; Hecate, the Greek goddess of enchantment, presides over rituals of natural magic. Both archetypal deities are associated with the Moon, darkness and the unknowable.

THOTH

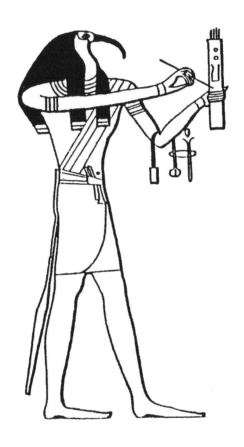

Praise to Thoth, the son of Ra,
The Moon, beautiful in his rising,
Lord of bright appearings,
Who illumines the gods.

Hail to thee, Moon, Thoth,
Who recalls all that is forgotten,
The rememberancer of time and eternity,
Whose words abide forever.

The verses were written by the pharaoh Haremhab, c. 1350 B.C., but the idea of a god representing wisdom and the power of speech had originated more than two thousand years earlier. The ibis-headed figure appears on Egypt's oldest monuments and his words are inscribed on walls and on papyrus scrolls found in the ancient tombs — for he is also credited with the art of writing. These records, collectively known as the Pyramid Texts and the Book of the Dead, form the Western world's oldest body of literature. The sacred texts are guidebooks for the soul's passage from death to renewal and Thoth leads the way. Myths, lore and legends repeated through the centuries present subtle concepts and spiritual achievements.

Together with his female counterpart — Maat, goddess of truth — Thoth guided Ra on the Sun god's daily journey from rise to set. The ancient Egyptians believed that Thoth reduced to words the will of an unknowable power and uttered the words in such a way that the universe sprang into being. As god of the Moon, "He who dispels darkness with his light," Thoth became recognized as the supreme master of magic, possessing all knowledge both human and divine. "Words of power" is a phrase occurring again and again in the Book of the Dead. Thoth presented Isis with words of power and she became known as "the Great Enchantress, Mistress of Magic, the Speaker of Spells." It wasn't enough merely to know the words, for to be effective they must be pronounced properly and in the correct tone of voice. Confidence and the ability to identify with the divinity was essential. A hymn of praise to Thoth is followed by a litany proclaiming: "I am Thoth, the lord of right and truth, I am

Thoth, the favored son of Ra, I am Thoth who giveth forth the speech of wisdom and understanding." To firmly believe that the deity has taken up residence within your heart will assure a favorable outcome of your desires.

Conviction and the power of words is further attested to in the Book of the Dead or the book of Coming Forth by Day, as Egyptians titled their mortuary manuals. This power is especially evident in the Negative Confession wherein all the sins never committed by the deceased are recited during the Last Judgement: I did not kill, I did not betray a friend, I did not abandon my family, among other declarations.

Egyptians considered the mind, heart and soul as one. The drawing below is a detail from the Papyrus of Ani, a scribe of c. 1500 B. C. The scene takes place in the Hall of Maat as her symbolic feather of Truth is weighed against Ani's heart. Ani stands expectantly at the far left. The jackal-headed Anubis supervises the scale as Thoth records the result. The baboon, a creature of high intelligence and long associated with Thoth, perches on top of the standard. As we can see, the trial goes well for Ani, because his heart is judged to be as light as a feather.

HECATE

And to my holy sacrifice invite,
The power who reigns in deepest hell and night;
I call Einodian Hecate, lovely dame,
Of earthly, watery, and celestial frame,
Sepulchral, in a saffron veil arrayed,
Pleased with dark ghosts that wander thru the shade.

A fragment from an Orphic Hymn invokes the ancient Greek goddess of night and magic. Einodia (the goddess who appears on the way) may have been a name by which Hecate was early known, for it suggests one of her archaic aspects as goddess of choice. Crossroads demand a decision and as the poet Theocritus wrote, "Where three roads meet, there she is standing." Romans so associated Hecate with crossroads that they called her Trivia — *tri*, three and *via*, road. The word is now synonymous with worthless knowledge — except, one might add, the comforting value of a venerable deity's guiding spirit.

Hesiod in Theogony (c. 8th century B. C.) relates that Zeus honored Hecate above all. She was the only child born to the Titans Perses and Asteria, and she retained her privilege when the Olympians came to power. Zeus "did her no wrong nor took anything away of all that was her portion among the former Titan gods." Hecate ruled the three realms of earth, heaven, and sea, and she bestowed upon or withheld from mortals any desired gift as she so willed. Hesiod adds that Zeus "made her a nurse of the young who saw the light of all-seeing Dawn."

The Athenians particularly worshipped Hecate as a patroness of families and children, and her statues were erected before the doors of houses. At the Hecatesia, celebrated monthly at dark of the moon, the rich provided a public supper set in the streets for the poorest citizens to enjoy.

It is a mystery how the benevolent goddess became the dread ruler of ghosts and demons, a denizen of the Underworld to whom evil spells were addressed. The slender crescent of the new moon and lighted torches became Hecate's emblems. Fierce black hounds accompanied her progress, their baying to strike terror in the hearts of lonely travelers. Yet the unknown writer of the beautiful Homeric Hymn to Demeter describes Hecate as "bright-coiffed" and "tender-hearted."

Memories of Hecate would persist in the archetypal witch figure, an unkempt crone muttering curses upon all who displeased her. Hecate's original image as the wise goddess of choice and chance shines again as Shakespeare provides her with speech in *Macbeth*:

ACT III.   SCENE V.
A heath.
Thunder. Enter the three WITCHES, *meeting*
HECATE.

FIRST WITCH.
Why, how now, Hecate! you look angerly.

HECATE.
Have I not reason, beldams as you are,
Saucy and overbold? How did you dare
To trade and traffic with Macbeth
In riddles and affairs of death;
And I, the mistress of your charms,
The close contriver of all harms,
Was never call'd to bear my part,
Or show the glory of our art?
And, which is worse, all you have done
Hath been but for a wayward son,

Spiteful and wrathful; who, as others do,

Loves for his own ends, not for you.

But make amends now: get you gone,

And at the pit of Acheron

Meet me i' the morning: thither he

Will come to know his destiny:

Your vessels and your spells provide,

Your charms, and every thing beside.

I am for th' air; this night I'll spend

Unto a dismal and a fatal end:

Great business must be wrought ere noon:

Upon the corner of the moon

There hangs a vaporous drop profound;

I'll catch it ere it come to ground:

And that, distill'd by magic sleights,

Shall raise such artificial sprites,

As, by the strength of their illusion,

Shall draw him on to his confusion:

He shall spurn fate, scorn death, and bear

His hopes 'bove wisdom, grace, and fear;

And you all know security

Is mortals' chiefest enemy.

[*Music & a song within, 'Come away, come away,'* & c.]

Hark! I am call'd; my little spirit, see,

Sits in a foggy cloud, and stays for me.   [Exit]

FIRST WITCH.

Come, let's make haste; she'll soon be back again. [Exeunt]

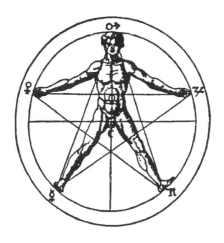

Esoteric Magic

Occult scholars often define magic as a means to dominate and command natural and supernatural forces. One such concept was born in the Hellenistic capital of Egypt at the turn of the Christian era. Alexandria attracted an intellectual community devoted to the supposition that human beings are potentially divine. Drawing inspiration from Egyptian wisdom, Greek philosophy, and Hebrew mysticism, a sect of thinkers developed a spiritual system of rational magic. Gnostic (to know) and Hermetic texts are attributed to Hermes Trismegistus (thrice greatest) in a hidden tribute to Thoth, the Egyptian god whose power was believed to surpass that of Hermes, the Greek god of eloquence.

Gnosticism and similar doctrines were driven underground by the rise of Christianity and Islamic conquest. The revival of mysticism during the European Renaissance blended with Roman Catholic ritual and the complex teachings of the Cabala, a magical work based on ancient Judaic traditions. In his book *Occult Philosophy*, the 16th-century scholar Agrippa advised his readers: "Therefore he that works in Magick must be of a constant belief, be credulous, and not at all doubt of obtaining the effect. For as a firm and strong belief doth work wonderful things, although it be in false works, so distrust and doubting doth dissipate and break the virtue of the mind of the worker."

The advent of printing spawned a series of volumes detailing the theory and practice of esoteric magic. The *grimoires*, or "black books" as they were called, restored a wealth of lost knowledge and the study continues to the present day. Words of power and the manner in which they are spoken form an integral part of novice training in many modern schools of metaphysical thought.

Natural Magic

Harmony with the cosmos describes the purpose of natural magic, which blends well with the sacred wisdom of ancient Egypt and the charm of Greek myth. Add to this an ephemeral quality so compelling and mysterious as to defy definition. Hidden aspects and subtle values compose its texture. One enters a world where nothing is quite as it seems — more enchanting and more lovely than can be supposed. Such a mystical atmosphere speaks to the heart.

Shakespeare in *A Midsummer Night's Dream* has Puck say:

> *And we fairies, that do run*
> *By the triple Hecate's team*
> *From the presence of the sun,*
> *Following darkness like a dream.*

The continuity of natural magic finds form in music and the power of the spoken word; evidence of the storyteller's art echoes down the centuries. When folklorists collected tales of fairies, elves, giants and witches, a common thread uniting them prevailed.

This literature's wellspring may be Ireland c. 3500 B. C., although no documents survive to chronicle the country's early lore. But the strange beauty of Old Irish poetry, kept alive by oral tradition, testifies to the presence of a civilization so old that even Homer seems recent by comparison. Another theory regarding the lore credits the Celtic and Teutonic tribes as they swept through Europe and the British Isles. The conquerors, refined by their contact with other cultures, became a moving tide of inspiration wherever they settled. Others believe that the gift of mystic awareness is simply a heritage passed down from generation to generation, its roots lost in the tangle of prehistory. Certain magic spells and incantations survive by the virtue of repetition and as an effective means to calm anxiety, renew hope, and give comfort to the human heart and soul.

Homage and Healing

In antiquity, a magic rite commonly began with a prelude —
the solemn tribute to a deity.

Ancient Egyptians hailed Thoth:

Hymns of praise to thee,
O thou god who makest the moment to advance,
Thou dweller among mysteries of every kind,
Thou guardian of the words which I speak.

Or a petitioner assumed the character of the god and
declared:

I am Thoth, whose hands are pure.
I am the lord of purity, destroyer of evil,
The scribe of right and truth,
And that which I abominate is sin.

Amulets to insure safety were inscribed with the lines:

May the blood of Isis, and the strength of Isis
be mighty to protect me and guard me from him
that would do unto me anything I abominate.

Osiris, supreme god of the netherworld, received the salutation:

Homage to thee, O creator of the gods,
Thou king of the North and of the South,
O Osiris, victorious one, ruler of the world
In thy gracious seasons;
Thou art lord of the celestial world.

Upon the rising of a new moon, symbol of Osiris risen from the dead, a suppliant faced north and recited a simple formula containing the essence of the Book of the Dead:

I am Yesterday, Today, and Tomorrow,
I have the power to be born a second time.

A primeval entreatment is addressed to the tree representing Nut, goddess of the heavens. Her mate Geb, the earth god, was portrayed in art as a goose and called the Great Cackler, from whose egg the world came into being. Hermopolis was the city of Thoth.

Hail, thou sycamore of the goddess Nut.
Grant me the water and air which dwell in thee.
    I have encircled the throne in Hermopolis,
I watch and guard the Egg of the Great Cackler.
It groweth, I grow;
It liveth, I live;
It breathes the air, I breathe the air.

In the final chapter of the Book of the Dead is a prayer to Amen, the "hidden" god who rose to prominence when

Thebes became capital of Egypt. The Theban priests endeavored to establish their local deity as lord of all the gods.

> *O Amen, O Amen, who art in heaven,*
> *Turn thy face upon the body of thy son*
> *And make him sound and strong.*

An appeal for fortitude in time of stress:

> *Horus, son of Isis! Strengthen thou me,*
> *According as thou hast strengthened thyself,*
> *Show thyself upon earth, O thou that returnest*
> *   and withdrawest thyself,*
> *And let thy will be done.*

As with the Egyptians, ancient Greeks were also provided with guidebooks to the afterlife. Texts derived from the Orphic mysteries were often engraved on leaf-shaped sheets of beaten gold and placed in tombs.

"Now you will find to the left of the halls of Hades a spring, and beside it a white cypress standing. Do not approach this spring. You will find on the other side a spring with guards before it. Say to them:

> *I am a child of Earth and Sky,*
> *Of heavenly race, you know it well:*
> *But I am parched with thirst, I perish.*

Give me, quickly, the cool water
From the Lake of Recollection.

And they shall give you to drink from the holy spring, and you will continue on the long, sacred way which other mystai gloriously walk."

The English Platonist Thomas Taylor published *The Mystical Hymns of Orpheus* in 1787. His translation and notes influenced the English Romantic poets and the American Transcendentalists. Taylor remarks that his study of the antiquities is "an inexhaustible treasure of intellectual wealth, and a perpetual fountain of wisdom and delight."

The legendary Orpheus set forth principles in his poetry that blended with the doctrines of Pythagoras to become the source of Orphism, an early Greek mystery religion. The Hymns are full of hidden meaning and signify divine concerns by symbols alone. Burning incense accompanied incantations of the Hymns; sweet-smelling herbs honored the moon goddess:

Fair lamp of Night, its ornament and friend,
Who givest to Nature's works their destined end.
Queen of the stars, all-wise Diana hail!
Decked with a graceful robe and shining veil;
Come, blessed Goddess, prudent, starry, bright,
Come moony-lamp with chaste and splendid light,
Shine on these sacred rites with prosperous rays,
And pleased accept thy suppliant's praise.

Frankincense scented the air when the south wind was summoned.

Wide coursing gales, whose lightly leaping feet
With rapid wings the air's wet bosom beat,
Approach benevolent, swift-whirling powers,
With humid clouds the principles of showers:
For showery clouds are portioned to your care,
To send on earth from all surrounding air.
Hear, blessed powers, these holy rites attend,
And fruitful rains on earth all-parent send.

Fumigation from manna, a sweet incense formed by flowers of ash trees, greeted Aesculapius, god of healing.

Great Aesculapius, skilled to heal mankind,
All-ruling Paean, and physician kind;
Whose arts medicinal, can alone assuage
Diseases dire, and stop their dreadful rage.

In classical literature Hecate's aid is called upon in casting magic spells. Euripides has Medea say:

Ah, by the Queen of Night, whom I revere
Above all, and for fellow-worker chose,
Hecate, dweller by mine hearth's dark shrine.

Theocritus has his heroine in Idyll II summon the moon goddess and Hecate:

Selene, shine brightly, for I will softly sing to you, goddess,
And to Hecate under the earth, before whom
 whelps tremble as she comes up
 thru the tombs of the dead and the black blood.
Hail, terrible Hecate! Attend me to the end.

Oral tradition has successfully sustained the mystic thought of the Old Irish culture in existence when the Egyptians built their pyramids. The ancient Irish blessed the rising sun:

Hail to thee, thou sun of the seasons,
As thou traverse the skies aloft;
Thy steps are strong on the wing of heaven,
Thou art the glorious mother of the stars.

The new moon was welcomed with similar reverence:

Greeting to you, new moon,
Kindly jewel of guidance!
I bend my knees to you,
I offer you my love.

37

To request good fortune for a beloved one:

> *Power of raven be thine,*
> *Power of eagle be thine,*
> *Power of storm be thine,*
> *Power of sun.*
> *Goodness of sea be thine,*
> *Goodness of earth be thine,*
> *Goodness of heaven.*
> *Each day be joyous to thee,*
> *No day be grievous to thee,*
> *Honor and compassion.*

Qualities of nature were called upon for strength:

> *I bind to myself today*
> *The swiftness of the wind,*
> *The power of the sea,*
> *The hardness of rocks*
> *The endurance of the earth.*

Norse shamans used a potent charm to combat evil and dismiss illness and pain. The words of power were chanted thrice as the sun rose.

> *Dropped the dew from the sky,*
> *From the stone, on the earth.*
> *As that dew vanishes, has vanished,*
> *Is blown away in the air, so may*
> *Thrice nine enchantments vanish,*
> *Perish in air and be blown away.*

An ancient Finnish magic song's refrain suggests that the burial mounds of ancestors were objects of devotion:

> *I call for help from the hill,*
> *I seek for folk from the hill.*

39

An incantation from the *Kalevala*, the medieval Finnish epic, invoked healing power.

O malady, disappear into the heavens:
Pain, rise up to the clouds:
Inflamed vapour, fly into the air,
In order that the wind may take thee away,
That the tempest may chase thee to distant regions,
Where neither sun nor moon give their light,
Where warm wind does not inflame the flesh.

The *Hávamál*, the great northern wisdom-poem in the Icelandic *Elder Edda*, has an injunction as to the gods:

Better no prayers than excessive offerings: a gift always seeks recompense. Better no offering than excessive sacrifice. So declared Thundr (Odin) before man's memory began.

Theurgy, the evocation of a divine spirit, developed from the Greek mysteries. It reached its height in Europe during the Renaissance, when sacraments interpreted by the Neoplatonists merged with Judaic-Christian doctrines. Such ceremonial magic began, as in ancient times, with praise to the deity. From the *Key of Solomon*:

O Lord, hear my prayer, let my cry come unto Thee,
O Lord God Almighty, who has reigned before the beginning
  of the Ages,
   and who by Thine infinite wisdom hast created
the heavens, the earth and the sea,
and all that is in them, visible and invisible, by a single word.

The rite ends as the evoked spirit is dismissed:

  By the Power of the Mighty Adonai, Elohim, Sabaoth,
  I license thee to depart, good spirit, whence thou came.
  Be ready to respond to my call when it shall please me.

The practice of esoteric magic was and is confined to the initiated few, but the power inherent in natural magic belongs to all. Folklore and household charms have brought peace of mind and healing to troubled hearts and spirits.

A Basque charm requires a glowing bed of coals and a handful of dried vervain herb to cast upon it as you declare:

> *Here is my pain,*
> *Take it and soar,*
> *Depart from me now,*
> *Offend me no more.*

An old Roman charm advises spitting on the ground, the fasting spittle is the most effective, and saying thrice:

> *O Earth, keep the pain,*
> *And health with me remain.*

A German spell to erase melancholy calls on the waning moon:

> *Like the moon from day to day,*
> *Let my sorrow wear away.*

Water collected from the ninth wave of an incoming tide has mystic elements. Thrice touch your forehead with the sea water as you say:

> *One for courage,*
> *Two for patience,*
> *Three for luck.*

Love and Divination

Youth is a time of eager anticipation. We long to know what life holds in store for us and in particular who will be our mate. Some very old charms are used to foretell the future.

On the first appearance of the new moon after spring equinox (March 21), go out in the evening and stand in a meadow. Greet the crescent moon and say:

> *All hail to the moon! all hail to thee!*
> *I prithee, good moon, declare unto me*
> *This night who my true love shall be!*

Go soon to bed and in your dreams the face of your future beloved will smile and beckon to you.

The waxing crescent moon as it sets in the west at twilight
is the primary focus for many divining chants.

> *Luna, every woman's friend,*
> *To me thy goodness condescend,*
> *Let this night in visions see*
> *Emblems of my destiny.*

Romany wisdom holds the full moon to be most powerful
in matters of love and future happiness.

> *Pray to the moon when she is round,*
> *Luck with you will then abound,*
> *What you seek for shall be found*
> *On the sea or solid ground.*

Others turn to the stars in hope of romantic fulfillment.

> *Star light, star bright,*
> *First star I see tonight,*
> *I wish I may, I wish I might,*
> *Have the wish I wish tonight.*

The Big and Little Dippers are the most familiar star patterns in the northern sky. Visible all year round, the ancients knew them as the Great and Small Bears (Ursa Major and Ursa Minor). The Big Dipper's seven stars are only part of the Great Bear. Draco, the Dragon, another large constellation, weaves in and around the two bears. The stars inspired an Old Irish wishing charm.

> *Great Bear, small bear,*
> *In the serpent winding;*
> *Hear now a simple prayer*
> *That love I may be finding.*

A classic summoning spell of witchcraft addresses the four compass points to evoke a lover. The encouraging refrain: *Even now he (or she) comes* is a continual source of hope. Folklorists call the repeated phrase a "run," characteristic of Celtic lore. Repetition of words in sequence, how-

47

ever, occurs in all cultures from the beginning. Egyptians murmured: *My heart, my mother; my heart, my mother! My heart of transformations* as a magical charm. The Greek poet Theocritus in the 3rd century B.C. uses the refrain: *Spin, magic wheel, and draw to me the man I love* in his Idyll II, The Love Charm.

Yarrow is a wild herb that grows all over the world. Its clusters of white flowers and feathery leaves evoke love and confidence. On finding the yarrow blooming in June, chant:

Yarrow, sweet yarrow, the first I have found,
In the name of the lady, I pluck from the ground;
As father loved mother and took her for his dear,
Tonight in a dream may my true love appear.

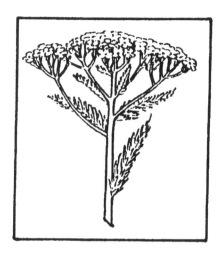

Choose a sprig of yarrow when the moon is new. Place it under your pillow and say:

> *Goodnight, fair yarrow,*
> *Thrice goodnight to thee;*
> *I hope before tomorrow's dawn*
> *My true love I shall see.*

An ancient folk charm of Scotland is recited in early summer under a waxing moon.

> *I will pick the smooth yarrow*
> *That my figure may be more elegant,*
> *That my lips may be warmer,*
> *That my voice may be more cheerful;*
> *May my voice be like a sunbeam,*
> *May my lips be like the juice of the strawberries.*

May I be an island in the sea,
May I be a hill on the land,
May I be a star when the moon wanes,
May I be a staff to the weak one;
   I shall wound every man,
   No man shall wound me.

In a lighter vein, pull petals from a daisy to divine the outcome of a romance to this chant:

One I love, two I love,
Three I love, I say,
Four I love with all my heart,
Five I cast away;

Six he loves, seven she loves,
Eight both love.
Nine he comes, ten he tarries,
Eleven he courts, twelve he marries.
Thirteen they quarrel,
Fourteen they part,
Fifteen he dies of a broken heart.

A similar means determines a lover's attitude based on the number of seeds found in an apple. Count them out in this order:

Loves me,
Longs for me,
Desires me,
Wishes me well,
Wishes me ill,
Does not care.

During an eclipse when the moon holds the sun in captivity, a maiden wishing to attract a particular lover lights a bright yellow candle at the darkest point of the event and repeats three times:

> *My lady hath thee in her thrall.*
> *I keep your light alive.*
> *Come now to me (name of person),*
> *She shall release thee to my sight.*

Concentrate on the desired object of your affections until the sun reappears. Allow the candle to burn down until it gutters out.

Another way to invite a dream of your future love calls on Thor, Norse god of thunder, and his potent hammer.

> *Hoping this night my true love to see,*
> *I place my shoes in the form of a T.*

A straying lover returns when frankincense is burned and knots are tied. In Virgil's poem *A Love Charm* from the Georgics;

I twist for thee even first of all these threads in number three,
In color threefold differing, and thrice about these altars
I draw thy lovely image: heaven delights in odd numbers.
            I am twining the bonds of Love.
O you my charms bring Daphnis from the town, bring Daphnis home.

Cast dried bay laurel leaves over burning coals to retrieve a lost lover. Repeat thrice:

Laurel leaves burn in fire,
Draw to me my heart's desire.

November Eve is a magical time of year. At midnight toss a ball of red wool as far as you can while holding the end of the skein firmly in your other hand. Reel in the wool and repeat the following lines:

I wind, I wind, my true love to find
The color of his hair, the clothes he will wear
On the day he is married to me.

A vision of your future mate will appear and wind along with you.

Dried leaves of vervain are scattered over a bed of glowing coals with this incantation:

It's not the herb that I now burn,
But my lover's heart I mean to turn,
May he no peace nor comfort find
Till he bends to me in soul and mind.

A gentler summoning spell is found in gypsy lore. Plant a flower bulb in a clean clay pot never before used. Repeat a beloved's name thrice. Chant:

As this root grows
And as its blossom blows,
May my true love's heart be
Softly turned unto me.

Nurture the plant with love and care to assure a happy outcome.

Candle spells divine the future of a romance. A glimpse ahead is always beneficial.

Light love's journey
With glow from thy flame,
Bring me a vision
Of joy or of pain.

A black candle on the left, a red candle in the middle, and a white candle on the right are lit as you whisper your lover's name.

By the light of candles three,
Golden flames reveal to me
A path, a sign, an omen fair
To guide me to my destiny.

Marriage, as we all know, is just a beginning. German folklore suggests that the bride coming home from the wedding must be the first to take hold of the house door. She will maintain mastery if she says:

> *This door I seize upon,*
> *Here all my will be done!*

Should the bridegroom overhear the spell, he may undo it by adding the words:

> *I grasp this knocker-ring,*
> *Be fist and mouth one thing!*

An ancient Anglo-Saxon rhyme makes a wise observation:

> *The hart he loves the high wood,*
> *The hare she loves the hill;*
> *The knight he loves his bright sword,*
> *The lady loves her will.*

Curses and Bewitchments

To have said is to have done!

The French magician Eliphas Levi defined the magic of language in this phrase. Duality of purpose is clearly apparent in another quote from Levi:

To affirm and will what ought to be is to create;
To affirm and will what ought not to be is to destroy.

Curses and blessings both require intensity and strength of will. A curse in ancient Egypt destroyed evil intent and magically protected the one for whom the spell was recited. The name of an enemy was written on a pottery bowl and smashed to pieces with the words:

May every evil word, evil speech, evil slander, evil thought, evil intrigue, evil fight, evil disturbance, evil plan or other evil thing, evil dream, or evil sleep of my enemy be reduced to fragments.

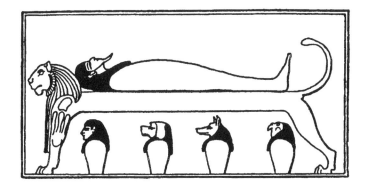

Curses inscribed on graves were directed toward violators of the sacred site and inspired a host of modern mystery dramas. The primary source was a warning of impending doom affixed to Tutankhamen's tomb:

Death will come on swift pinions to those
who dare disturb the rest of the Pharaoh.

The threat was borne out when more than twenty people connected with the excavation at various times died under curious circumstances. Archaeologists ascribed the events to mere coincidence, but the world press delighted in the chilling legend.

Another tomb cursed the violator with a terrifyingly portentous threat:

He shall hunger! He shall thirst!
He shall faint! He shall sicken!

Egyptologist Margaret A. Murray's fame rests on her ingenious theory that witchcraft springs from an ancient form of spiritual belief. Her classic work, *The Witch-Cult in*

Western Europe, is regarded as an essential factor in the establishment of Wicca as a bona fide religious expression. Less well known is her survey of Egyptian culture, *The Splendor That Was Egypt*, in which Dr. Murray writes:

"One of the most tremendous curses is the curse pronounced against the enemies of Ra, who is here identified with the Pharaoh. Certain magical ceremonies must be performed, and then come the words:

Burning be on you! They shall have no souls thereby, nor spirits nor bodies nor shades nor magic nor bones nor hair nor utterances nor words. They shall have no grave thereby, nor house nor hole nor tomb. They shall have no garden thereby, nor tree nor bush. They shall have no water thereby, nor bread nor light nor fire. They shall have no children thereby, nor family nor heirs nor tribe. They shall have no head thereby, nor arms nor legs nor gait nor seed. They shall have no seats on earth thereby.... Their souls shall not be permitted to come out of the Netherworld and they shall not be among those who live upon earth, on no day shall they behold Ra, but they shall be bound and fettered in Hell in the lower Netherworld and their souls shall not be permitted to come forth for ever and ever."

The ancient Hebrews have no peer in devising words to blast an enemy. Psalm 109, the "Cursing Psalm," demands a fit punishment of the wicked.

HOLD not thy peace, O God of my praise; for the mouth of the wicked and the mouth of the deceitful are opened against me: they have spoken against me with a lying tongue.

They compassed me about also with words of hatred; and fought against me without a cause.

For my love they are my adversaries: but I give myself unto prayer.

And they have rewarded me evil for good, and hatred for my love.

Set thou a wicked man over him: and let Satan stand at his right hand.

When he shall be judged, let him be condemned: and let his prayer become sin.

Let his days be few; and let another take his office.

Let his children be fatherless, and his wife a widow.

Let his children be continually vagabonds, and beg: let them seek their bread also out of their desolate places.

Let the extortioner catch all that he has; and let strangers spoil his labor.

Let there be none to extend mercy unto him: neither let there be any to favor his fatherless children.

Let his posterity be cut off; and in the generation following let their names be blotted out.

Let the iniquity of his fathers be remembered with the Lord; and let not the sin of his mother be blotted out.

Let them be before the Lord continually, that he may cut off the memory of them from the earth.

Because that he remembered not to show mercy, but persecuted the poor and needy man, that he might even slay the broken in heart.

As he loved cursing, so let it come unto him: as he delighted not in blessing, so let it be far from him.

As he clothed himself with cursing like as with his garment, so let it come into his bowels like water, and like oil into his bones.

Let it be unto him, as the garment which covereth him, and for a girdle wherewith he is girded continually.

Let this be the reward of mine adversaries from the Lord, and of them that speak evil against my soul.

But do thou for me, O God the Lord, for thy name's sake: because thy mercy is good, deliver thou me.

For I am poor and needy, and my heart is wounded within me.

I am gone like the shadow when it declineth: I am tossed up and down as the locust.

My knees are weak through fasting; and my flesh faileth of fatness.

I became also a reproach unto them: when they looked upon me they shook their heads.

Help me O Lord my God: O save me according to thy mercy:

that they may know that this is thy hand; that thou, Lord, hast done it.

Let them curse, but bless thou: when they arise, let them be ashamed; but let thy servant rejoice,

Let mine adversaries be clothed with shame; and let them cover themselves with their own confusion, as with a mantle.

I will greatly praise the Lord with my mouth; yea, I will praise him among the multitude.

For he shall stand at the right hand of the poor, to save him from those that condemn his soul.

Greeks of ancient times resorted to incising the name of an adversary on a lead tablet, binding it with wire, and burying it in the ground with these words of commitment:

Deep in the earth I bury your evil ways.

I bind you in tongue and soul from this day on.

Occasionally a spell was so strong that its effects lasted beyond the grave for generations. Romans believed that cursed, tormented souls, caught by an evil force that held them captive somewhere between life and death, were condemned to wander about the earth causing terror as apparitions. To pacify them, a festival called the Lemuria was held in the month of May. The solemnities continued for three nights, during which time people threw black beans on the graves of the deceased and beat drums and kettles, muttering these magic words thrice each night:

Go hence, ghosts of my ancestors.

When Reginald Scot wrote *The Discoverie of Witchcraft* in 1584, his intention was to expose the absurdity of that era's witch mania. His work, however, became a primary source for the study of the Black Arts. Scot revealed a magician's secret for dealing with a troublesome ghost:

By the mysteries of the deep, by the flames of Banal, by the power of the East, and by the silence of the night, by the holy rites of Hecate, I conjure and exorcise thee, thou distressed Spirit, to present thyself here, and reveal unto me the cause of thy calamity, why thou didst offer violence to thy own liege life, where thou art now in being, and where thou wilt hereafter be.

A way to punish an enemy and be delivered from evil at the same time is dutifully recorded in Scot's book:

"Upon the Sabbath day before sunrising, cut a hazel wand saying, *I cut thee, O bough of this summer's growth,*
    In the name of whom I mean to beat or maim.
Then cover a table with carpet, and say;
    In nomine patris et filii et spiritus sancti ter.
And striking thereon say as follows (English it he that can),
    Drochs myrroch, esenaroth beta baruch asi maaroth.
And then say,
    Holy trinity punish him that hath wrought this mischief, and take it away by thy great justice, eson, elion, emaris, ales, age;
And strike the carpet three times with your wand."

With the rise of Christianity, the Lord's Prayer, the Pater-noster, became a magic formula. Foes of the faith reversed the letters of the Latin prayer to create what came to be known as the Devil's Creed:

Nema. Olam a son arebil des

Menoitatnet ni sacudni son en te

Sirtson subirotibed

Sumittimid son te tucis artson

Atibed sibon ettimid te

Eidoh sibon ad

Munaiditoc murtson menap

Arret ni to oleoc ni

Tucis aut satnulov tail

Muut munger tainevda

Muut nemon rutecifitcnas

Sileac ni iuq

Retson retap.

In *The Return of the Native,* Thomas Hardy also describes casting a spell by turning about Christendom's holiest prayer.

"It was a strange jargon — the Lord's Prayer repeated backwards — the incantation usual in proceedings for obtaining unhallowed assistance against an enemy. Susan uttered the lugubrious discourse three times slowly."

Amen. Evil from us deliver but temptation into not us lead and us against trespass who those forgive we as trespasses our us forgive and bread daily our day this us give. Heaven in is it as earth on, done be will thy, come kingdom thy, name thy be hallowed, heaven in art who father our.

The chants accompanied the pronouncement of the name and sin of the evil-doer. The incantations may have served another purpose. Sound alone, especially unintelligible sound, is an archaic aid to deep concentration. Mindless verbal repetition is an effective way to erase conscious thought. An old occult adage cryptically advises:

> *If ye would clear the path to will,*
> *Make certain that the mind be still.*

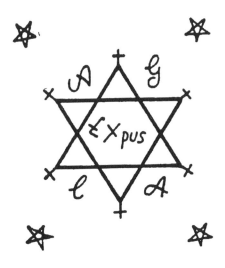

An eerie curse is found in the infamous *Grimorium Verum*, a sorcerer's handbook studied throughout Europe during the 19th century.

"TO NAIL AN ENEMY

Go to a cemetery, remove nails from an old coffin, saying:

Nails, I take you, so that you may serve to turn aside and cause evil to all persons whom I will. In the name of the Father, and of the Son, and of the Holy Spirit. Amen.

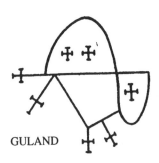

GULAND

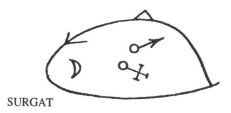

SURGAT

When you wish to use it, you must look for a footprint of your enemy and making the three figures of GULAND,

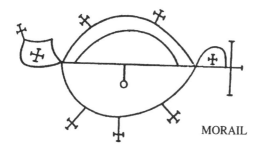

MORAIL

SURGAT and MORAIL, fix the nail in the middle saying:

Paternoster upto in terra.

Hit the nail with a stone, saying:

Cause evil to (name of the cursed), until I remove thee.

Re-cover the place with a little dust, and remember it well, because one cannot remove the evil which this causes, but by removing the nail, and saying:

I remove thee, so that the evil which thou has caused shall cease. In the name of the Father, and of the Son, and of the Holy Spirit. Amen.

Then take the nail out, and efface the characters: not with the same hand as you make them, but with the other. Thus it will be without danger."

In the world of magic, a talisman, especially one prepared by the practitioner, has within its composition forces for good and for evil. The duality of intent is a theme evident in fairy lore. Edwin S. Hartland's *The Science of Fairy Tales* notes: *"I will give you for gift* are words fairies make use of when they have a mind to do good or harm to anybody. The charge is always the same whether the gift brings joy or sorrow."

Knots are potent tools in magic. The Greek word *katadesmoi* literally means "bindings" and also refers to magic spells. An early 20th-century Dream Book by an unknown author advises caution before working a spell of revenge.

"Be certain of the identity of someone you suspect is ill-wishing you. The forces you release on an innocent person can turn against you. Before taking action, tie nine knots in a one-foot-length of scarlet yarn as you say:

These knots I knot, to know the thing
I know not yet, that I may see
The one who is my enemy.

Sleep with the charm under your pillow and a vision of that person who means you harm will appear in a dream."

No other binding talisman illustrates the dualistic theme more surely than the Witches' Ladder. An ancient charm Italian witches call *la guirlanda delle streghe*, "the witches' garland" and a powerful *baka* in Voodoo, the feather wreath can promote good or provoke misfortune. The rite of prepa-

ration is identical; only the ingredients differ. A dark version of The Witches' Ladder from a Welsh source proffers guidance in its creation.

"If your intent is vengeance, collect nine feathers from either the crow, raven, owl, peacock or black cock. Plait into one cord three stands of black yarn of about three feet in length, tie off one end and knot the feathers into the braid, as evenly spaced as possible. Visualize the person for whom the gift is intended and the fate you wish upon them. As you work the spell, chant the progression in this way:

> *Tie one, the spell's begun.*
> *Tie two, no power undo.*
> *Tie three, so shall it be.*
> *Tie four, forever more.*
> *Tie five, the charm's alive.*
> *Tie six, its magic fix.*
> *Tie seven, now under heaven.*
> *Tie eight, work winds of fate.*
> *Tie nine, to my design.*

Tie together both ends of the braided cord to form a circle. Place the wreath where your enemy is sure to find it."

Occult writer and witch Sybil Leek offered a way to repel a curse:

"This is a very simple incantation and should be repeated three times when the moon is waning. It is sometimes called the Witches' Formula.

> *By the power of fire,*
> *By the power of earth,*
> *By the power of air,*
> *By the power of water,*
> *By the life in the blood,*
> *Be thou (name the person) stopped.*
> *Let the evil return to whence it cometh.*
> *Let thy words be unto thee*
> *As thou would have them be to me.*
> *I banish you. So mote it be."*

A popular way to defeat an opponent is to place a scrap of paper bearing his or her name under an ice-cube tray in the refrigerator. The words may have once been runes in northern climes:

> *I place you in a prison of ice.*
> *Be chilled till I release you.*

Oddities and Adages

Incomprehensible invocations and chants in an unknown language are prevalent in Western magical tradition.

To determine guilt or innocence, the medieval magus Peter of Abano recommended a formula of six words "understood neither by those who speak them nor by others." Suspects were named and the conjuration uttered compelled a demon to come forth and identify the culprit.

> *Dies*
>
> *Mies*
>
> *Jeschet*
>
> *Benedoefet*
>
> *Dowima*
>
> *Enitemaus*

From Jacob Grimm's vast collection of posthumous notes are what he terms as "words of great magic power."

berlicke, berlocke! policke, polucke, podrei! (German)

brelique, breloque! berlik berloc! (French)

perljk tudes! (Bohemian)

Odd conjure words occur in American folklore as evidenced by a tale of Vance Randolph in *Ozark Superstitions:*

"A big yellow cat once walked into a cabin where I was sitting with an aged tie hacker and his wife. The woman began to shout 'Witch! Witch!' at the top of her voice. The old man sprang up, crossed the fingers of both hands, and chanted something that sounded like *'Pulley-bone holy ghost double-yoke! Pulley-bone holy ghost double-yoke!'* The cat walked in a wide circle past the hearth, stared fixedly at the old gentleman for a moment, and then strolled out across the threshold. We followed a moment later, but the animal was nowhere in sight. It may have crawled under the cabin, or under a corncrib which stood only a few yards away, but the old couple insisted that it had vanished by reason of some supernatural dispensation."

To summon up one's own power, the Finns cried out:

nouse luontoni, surge vis mea!

Teutonic knights in time of peril prayed not to a god:

so mir ih! (So help me I myself.)

One oddity in particular is singular in its longevity:

Eko, Eko, Azarak!

Eko, Eko, Zomelak!

Bagabi laca bachabe

Lamac cahi achababe

Karrelyos

Lamac lamec Bachalyas

Cabahagy sabalyos

Baryolos
Lagoz atha cabyolas
Samahac et famyolas
Harrahya.

With the exception of the first two lines, the conjuration comes from a 13th-century play by the celebrated French poet Rutebeuf. The chant is spoken today as part of an initiation rite by members of certain sects practicing modern witchcraft.

The English literary detective Michael Harrison linked the words to the archaic Basque tongue — not only the oldest European language, but one unrelated to any other on Earth. Rutebeuf, his name a pseudonym, may have been Basque. Harrison's efforts suggest the chant celebrated the November Eve festival. And if this is so, its place in witchcraft makes perfect sense, for Halloween is the most sacred holiday of witches.

An old English folk rhyme contains some odd lines:

> Hey ho for Halloween!
> When the witches will be seen,
> Some in black, and some in green,
> Hey ho for Halloween!
> *Horse and hattock, horse and go,*
> *Horse and pellatis, ho! ho!*

A Scottish legend collected by the 17th-century antiquarian John Aubrey in his *Miscellanies* mentions the phrase.

"An ancestor of the then Lord Duffus was walking in the fields near his house in Morayshire when he heard the noise of a whirlwind and of voices crying *Horse and Hattock!* This was the exclamation fairies were said to use when they remove from any place. Lord Duffus was bold enough to cry *Horse and Hattock* also, and was immediately caught up through the air with the fairies."

Jacob Grimm notes: "An English spell for faring to Elfland is *horse and hattock! with my top!*"

Isobell Gowdie's freely given testimony during her trial for witchcraft in 1662 is a virtual treatise on Scottish folklore: "When we would ride, we take windle-straws, of beanstalks, and put them betwixt our feet, and say thrice:

> *Horse and hattock, horse and go,*
> *Horse and pellattis, ho! ho!*

And immediately we fly away wherever we would."

Witches are as renowned as fairies for flying through the air. The woodcut above appeared in incunabula (books printed before 1501) and was titled by its author "Departure for the Sabbath." One of the earliest depictions of their flight, these witches rode a fork rather than a broomstick and were costumed as an ass, a hawk and a calf. As the fairies, witches also relied on magic words to carry them aloft. Among Jacob Grimm's copious notes on folklore: "They (witches) anoint a stick with the words:

Away we go, not too high and not too low."

Yorkshire's famous witch and prophetess, Mother Shipton chanted the magic words:

Updraxi, call Stygician Helluic!

Sometimes the language is understandable while the original meaning is lost. This occurs often in nursery rhymes, a treasury of arcane lore.

> *Ladybug, Ladybug,*
> *Fly away home,*
> *Your house is on fire,*
> *Your children will burn.*

The familiar childhood chant was once "a charm to speed the sun across the dangers of sunset, the house on fire symbolizing the red evening sky" according to folklorists Iona and Peter Opie.

A beautiful verse from early Anglo-Saxon times may have been a protection spell:

> *Gray goose and gander,*
> *Waft your wings together,*
> *And carry the good king's daughter*
> *Over the one-strand river.*

Elizabethan dramatists Thomas Middleton in *The Witch* (Act V, Scene III) and Shakespeare in *Macbeth* (Act IV, Scene I) both use the same strange song. Rather than borrowing from each other, scholars have concluded that the chant was "in all probability, a traditional one."

> *Black spirits and white, red spirits and gray,*
> *Mingle, mingle, mingle, you that mingle may!*
> > *Titty, Tiffin,*
> > *Keep it stiff in;*
> > *Firedrake, Puckey,*
> > *Make it lucky;*
> > *Liard, Robin,*
> > *You must bob in.*
> *Round, around, around, about, about!*
> *All good come running in, all ill keep out!*

Household sayings we hear as children often become words of power that echo through time to guide our daily living. The principles of wisdom and truth set forth in these concise verbal expressions represent the basic concepts of magical practice.

The moving tide reveals the truth.

Joy is as inevitable as sorrow.

Secrets are best hidden in plain sight.

Evil done returns to the sender thrice.

Good done comes back one hundredfold.

Thoughts are things.

Leave hatred to those not strong enough to love.

Know your limits and remain within them.

Guard hope as you would the last flame.

To judge is to harm.

Life is nature's gift.

A will unused is a will undone.

The weak shape their own destiny.

As above, so below.

Every thing involves its opposite, for all is one.

Least said, easiest mended.

If you would learn to dance, never watch your feet.

There is but one of you in all of time.

You cannot learn what you think you already know.

A creature in distress is a sacred object.

Never use a razor to cut wood.

Pure ends require pure means.

Only you know what's good for you.

Need not who needs not thee.

Enough is better than too much.

Believe you have it, and you have it.

The guilty flee where no one pursues.

Lose not substance for shadow.

The Uses of Silence

Silence has ever been a part of magical tradition in the West. "Speak not lest ye break the spell" is a familiar warning in fairy tales. Eliphas Levi, the renowned ceremonial magician, listed the rules of the Magus: to know, to dare, to will, to keep silence. The earliest testimony to the power of silence is a prayer to Thoth, the Egyptian Lord of Magic:

O thou sweet Well for the thirsty in the desert!
It is closed up for him who speaks,
But it is open for him who keeps silence.
When he who keeps silence comes,
Lo he finds the Well.

Volume IV of Jacob Grimm's *Teutonic Mythology* contains an appendix of spells and superstitions taken down from the speech of common people all over Europe. Grimm believed the collected folklore to be a survival of a once dominant religion. Silence is a persistent theme:

He that would dig up a treasure, must not speak a word.

If you have a swollen neck, go in silence to the mill, steal the tie from one of the sacks, and tie it about your neck.

On Matthias night (February 24) the young people meet, the girls plait one wreath of periwinkle, one of straw, and as a third thing carry a handful of ashes; at midnight they go silently to a running water on which the three things are to float. Silent and blindfold, one girl after another dances about the water, then clutches at a prognostic, the periwinkle meaning a bridal wreath, the straw misfortune, the ashes death.

If a baby cries much in the first six weeks, pull it through a piece of unboiled yarn three times in silence. If that does no good, let the mother, after being churched, go home in silence, undress in silence, and throw all her clothes on the cradle backwards.

Spinsters on St. John's Eve twine a wreath of nine sorts of flowers, and try to throw it backwards and in silence on to a tree. As often as it falls, so many years will they remain unmarried.

In setting peas, take a few in your mouth before sunset, keep them in silently while planting, and those you set will be safe from sparrows.

Water drawn downstream and in silence, before sunrise on Easter Sunday, does not spoil, and is good for anything.

A piece of oak passed lightly over the body in silence, before sunrise of John's day, heals all open sores.

To discover what the year shall bring, they plant themselves on a cross-roads or parting of the ways at 12 the night before Christmas, stand stockstill without speaking for an hour, whilst all the future opens on their eyes and ears. This they call "to go hearken."

The magic of silence reached America with the early settlers. A custom of holding a Dumb Supper survived among hillfolk of Arkansas and Missouri. *Ozark Superstitions* by Vance Randolph supplies a description of the ritual.

"In some sections of Arkansas, the girls 'set a dumb supper,' by making a pone of cornmeal and salt, in complete silence. Each girl must take her turn at stirring the meal, each must shift the pone as it bakes; each must place a piece of the bread on her own plate, and another on the plate next to hers at the table. When this is done, the girls open the doors and windows, then sit down silently and bow their heads. All during the baking, the wind has grown stronger, and by this time there should be a regular gale blowing through the house. Often the lights are blown out. The phantom husbands are supposed to enter in silence. Each girl is supposed to recognize the man who sits down beside her. If she sees nobody, it means she will never marry. If she sees a black figure, without recognizable features, it means that she will die within a year. Many people still take this business seriously enough to forbid their daughters to trifle with it. Some parents say it ain't Christian and smells of witchcraft, while others object to such foolishness because it sometimes frightens girls into hysteria."

Love and magic are akin. Both arts may be learned but not taught. Neither rely on reason, nor can their power or beauty be readily explained. Silence proves to be beneficial to both.

> *Explanation by the tongue*
> *Makes most things clear.*
> *But love unexplained*
> *Is better.*
> — JALAL AL-DIN RUMI

> *Never seek to tell thy love,*
>   *Love that never told can be;*
> *For the gentle wind doth move*
>   *Silently, invisibly.*
> — WILLIAM BLAKE

> *The deepest feeling always*
>   *Shows itself in silence.*
> — MARIANNE MOORE